NUGGETS
BY DAY
— and —
GEMS
BY NIGHT

Dr. Melinger
Thank you for your
leadership and
mentoring this
year!

Nuggets by DAY and Gems by NIGHT

Thoughts and Insights from the Mind of
Bishop Rudolph McKissick

BISHOP RUDOLPH W. McKISSICK, Jr.

NUGGETS BY DAY AND GEMS BY NIGHT

Cover Design by Atinad Designs

© Copyright 2009

SAINT PAUL PRESS, DALLAS, TEXAS
First Printing, 2009

The name SAINT PAUL PRESS and its logo are registered as a trademark in the U.S. patent office.

ISBN-13: 978-0-9819672-5-7

Printed in the U.S.A.

Dedication

I dedicate this book first and foremost to God, Who for His own reasons, and in spite of my imperfections, called me to minister His perfect Word. God deserves all glory and praise. I also want to dedicate this book to my parents, Dr. and Mrs. Rudolph W. McKissick, Sr. It has been said that you can choose your friends, but you can't choose your family. I thank God for making the choice for me. My father is my model as well as my parent. I am so grateful to be able to not only work with him but to also watch him with the dignity and pastoral heart that makes him without peer. Finally, to three men who now live in glory but impacted my consciousness about ministry more than any others: Dr. Samuel DeWitt Proctor, Dr. Miles Jones, and my father-in-law, Dr. Paul Nichols.

Contents

Foreword
by Dr. William H. Curtis

It is no secret to anyone who has heard Dr. Rudolph McKissick preach that he is undoubtedly one of the truly gifted preachers of this generation. His keen exegetical eye and theological depth have blessed congregants in churches across the country for a number of years. He fights hard to remain faithful to the integrity of a biblical passage and the African American lens through which he sees scripture explains his social hermeneutic. He is one of the complete ministry packages.

Dr. Evans Crawford who taught me preaching at Howard University Divinity School commented after hearing my senior sermon that it lacked but one thing, pain! He went on to say that it was not my fault that the sermon lacked this so noticeably. He assured me then what I have come to know now, that maturity and experiences would season the sermons I would preach with enough pain to impact the human heart.

Dr. McKissick has produced this devotional after being forced to wed his preaching to perhaps one of the most painful times in his life. To live with the fear of whether he would be able to preach again walked him reluctantly into a season of solitude and spiritual introspection. This explains the depth of thought found in this devotional, the intimate relationship that is evident between him and God as well as the theological musing that shapes both the themes and content of the daily entries.

I pray that persons will be blessed by Dr. McKissick's reservoir of biblical knowledge, pastoral experience, large net of relationships, and more importantly, his ponderings from places of ministry, anguish, and fulfillment. You indeed will develop a closer relationship with the Lord.

I Pray for Your Growth,

–Dr. William H. Curtis
Pastor, Mount Ararat Baptist Church
Pittsburgh, Pennsylvania

$\mathcal{D}$AY ONE

 WHEN YOU FEEL INSECURE ALWAYS
REMEMBER YOU WERE CHOSEN BY GOD
EVEN WHEN YOU WERE NOT
CONSIDERED BY PEOPLE.

GEM:
HYPOCRITICAL HOLINESS
Written in the days after the election of Barack Obama

I just finished reading a great and provocative book entitled: *I'm Fine With God...It's Christians I Can't Stand.* As I have listened on television and seen in captions on Facebook and MySpace, I now concur with that author. It amazes me how some Christians can talk one way, but when things don't go their way, they turn into arrogant, high and mighty judges. One of the quotes I read from someone who was not for President Obama said, "God bless America...even though we don't deserve it." So I guess we deserve God to damn us? To be damned or undeserving of God's blessing is the opposite of blessing from God the Divine. These same Christians demonized a preacher for saying, "God damn America," but they can imply the very same sentiment with spiritual platitudes and it is okay because it suits their hypocritical view.

One of the chapters in the book is called, "I Can't Stand Christians Who Think They are Correctly Right and Everyone Else Is Wrongly Left." How true it is. Many will stand on what they call biblical morality in taking a stand against abortion because it's murder. It is interesting to me that they claim that Mosaic standard at the beginning of life but don't mind killing them through capital punishment in the middle of their life. If they are so biblical what happened to grace? These same persons accepted God's grace through Jesus because they believed by confessing Jesus that WHATEVER was in THEIR past could be erased and FORGIVEN.

Many of us have been forgiven for things that should have landed us in jail. We just did not get caught and were able to plead the blood of Jesus and the mercy of God through Jesus Christ. To suggest that one can get caught breaking the law, go to jail as a consequence, but be beyond experiencing the grace of God to the point that even if they repent while in the jail and turn their life around to become a witness for the Kingdom and become productive in the country is not worth letting them live is the height of hypocrisy and dangerously close to playing God. To be against abortion but for capital punishment is tantamount to saying let them live when they are born (and I DO agree), but it's okay to kill them later on. How hypocritical. I guess that does not apply to everyone. If God is in control, then God has allowed this moment in time. He has not allowed it as punishment. To suggest that, makes you as bad as other preachers who boldly but sadly suggested that 9/11 was God's punishment against certain cities (i.e. New York) for homosexuality (I guess they got left off of the report about preachers who said things about 9/11).

Be careful my Christian brothers and sisters. Hypocrisy is not a good look. If you can't be spiritually mature enough to accept what God allows, then at least be patriotic enough to show appreciation for the moment of history. At least celebrate the fact that something that was never intended to happen when Blacks as a people were brought from the coasts of Africa has happened in our lifetime. Celebrate the fact that the vision God gave that Ebony emancipator, Dr. Martin Luther King, Jr., was not a figment of his imagination. God showed him the dream, America caught the dream and now the dream is becoming a reality. Celebrate the fact that this is proof that no label can limit you—not black, not woman, not minority, not uneducated. No label can be placed upon you that you cannot overcome. Celebrate what your ancestors said no to, God and votes said yes to. I would not be presumptuous enough to say this is God's intentional will. I do not know the ways of God. Isaiah warns me of being arrogant enough to think I know God that well. But I do know that it is what God has allowed and we can learn from what God allows and accept it as God's will for His own reasons. Be holy enough to respect that and patriotic enough to celebrate it.

$\mathcal{D}$AY TWO

MORNING NUGGET REMEMBER THIS: GOD CAN USE STRUGGLES TO BRING OUT OF YOU SOMETHING THAT IS IN YOU THAT ONLY A STRUGGLE CAN PRODUCE.

GEM:
LIBERATION THEOLOGY
Try to understand it before you bash it

One of the things that came out during the presidential campaign was how many have no appreciation or PROPER UNDERSTANDING of Liberation Theology. More often than not, you would hear persons comparing it to and actually calling it Marxism. It is amazing to me that black theology or liberation theology can be called Marxism when in reality the premise of liberation theology is close to what Republicans CLAIM to espouse and that is, liberating people from oppressive mentalities and oppressive obstructions in an effort to be liberated and empowered to be all God created them to be. That, my friends, is the premise of liberation theology. It is not racist, because it does not claim or declare that one group of people is better than another group of people.

God created each of us in His image, but there have been obstructions, intentional and unintentional, that have not allowed some to walk in the fullness and freedom of their Divine design. While you may not particularly like the words or phrases some may use, look beyond those words to see the point they are trying to make. Do not sum up the theology that has gotten blacks through slavery and racism by defining it through the tainted lens of video shots that are out of context. Do not downplay a theology that is the encouragement even still today not only of African Americans, but of other groups of people who are considered least, last and left out, in many instances.

We can all discuss very vociferously our differences on policies and the like, but to spew the poison of character assassination that has gone on by many is astounding. Let me remind you of the words of Jesus on that mountainside as He spoke into the lives of His disciples when He said, "JUDGE NOT SO THAT YOU DON'T GET JUDGED." The danger of self-righteousness is that there is this sense of entitlement to point to the forgiveness of God through Jesus Christ and how the blood of Jesus Christ makes forgiveness possible when we confess our sins.

If forgiveness works in one camp then apply it to all camps. To compare a theology to communism without knowing much about it is a dangerous game. Somebody needs to tell many of the pundits that if their statements are true then that means they also have a problem with preachers who seek to open the eyes of people to that which obstructs them in order for them to be free to live. Sounds like slavery to me. I abhor racism. I think it is sick.

It is sinful. It is dysfunctional. I hate any "ism", be it sexism or ageism. But what is even worse is parading in the name of morality and Christianity and not letting what comes out of your mouth match what you claim to practice in your life.

$\mathcal{D}$AY THREE

 REMEMBER THAT YOUR POTENTIAL SPEAKS TO YOU OF YOUR TOMORROW IN SPITE OF YOUR YESTERDAY.

GEM:

BLESSED
Condition or Consciousness

It is without a doubt that we live in a society that is now driven by levels of materialism. We determine the length, depth and width of a person's importance by the amount of material gain he or she shows. This philosophy has now, unfortunately, found its way into the church. WE have been living through an oppressive move called "prosperity." It becomes the sign of how "blessed" we really are. The suggestion of this premise is that God desires you to be rich and as a consequence the barometer of just how pleased God is with you and how blessed you are can be seen in the amount of material gain you have in your life. As a result, persons now flock to ministries where they can be "taught" (and I use that term quite loosely) how to walk in material gain, i.e. prosperity, and how this now becomes a sign of the favor of God upon your life. My issue is not the idea of prosperity. There is nothing wrong with WORKING, SOWING, TITHING and God blessing your OBEDIENCE AND GOOD MANAGEMENT to put you in such a position where you are able to purchase the "finer things of life." My issue is not prosperity but premise. To suggest that how much God is pleased with an individual is manifested or evidenced in how much they have eliminates many who have been faithful to God, even unto death, but did not have much. It flies in the face of the teaching of Jesus.

It was a widow woman who had nothing more than a mite who received the commendation from Jesus in the temple. It was a poor teenage girl who was chosen to be the vessel to carry the greatest gift ever given or known to humanity- Jesus Christ Himself. What do you say to the old church mother who has been faithful to God by tithing and serving but is not rolling in cash or cars? Do we suggest to her that her faith is not strong enough? What do we say to the brother who is a faithful servant to the Kingdom, active in the church, but gets laid off and has trouble making ends meet? Has God become displeased with Him on some level? To be blessed is not a condition, but rather is a consciousness. Being blessed is a state of being that begins with a proper understanding of who you are and Whose you are. You are not necessarily blessed because you have thousands of dollars in the bank, fancy cars to choose from, and name brands on every piece of clothing you own; that may mean that you are rich or that you have good credit, but you are not necessarily blessed.

Sadly, too many Christians are running around looking to climb the ladder of the "blessed life" through material gain.

Beloved, the blessed life is in knowing God through Jesus Christ and knowing who you are and Whose you are. It is knowing that with all your flaws and faults you are still God's child. It is not a condition of existence, but rather a state of consciousness. No money, but I'm blessed because I am God's child; driving the same car from 1999, but I am blessed because I am God's child. Do not get me wrong: learn to invest, learn to save, and put yourself in a position to never have to borrow. And if that does not happen to the level of some preacher's definition of being blessed, hold your head up and walk like a millionaire, because if you belong to God and know who you are, you are truly blessed.

$\mathcal{D}$AY FOUR

MORNING NUGGET GOD'S PROMISES ARE CLEAR EVEN WHEN THE PROCESS GETS CLOUDY. REMEMBER WHAT GOD TOLD YOU IN SPITE OF WHAT YOU GO THROUGH.

GEM: SENSE FROM SURGERY

Shakespeare once said that there are sermons in stones, so I thought I would give you some sense from my surgery. It was in August of 2008 that I underwent a very extensive surgery on my spine. I was sidelined and confined for close to four months as I sought to recover and get back into, as my father often says, the "normal walks of life." As I reflect on the process of this surgery, some spiritual truths came into my mind that I would like to share with you.

The first thing that popped into my mind was how they discovered there was a problem. I was having tingling and numbness in my left arm and hand. I was displaying symptoms but did not know what was causing it. I knew that something was wrong but did not have the expertise to come to a conclusion about my condition. I had to admit that something was wrong and go to someone who had the knowledge to discover what it was. Such is the way of life. We can often know something is not right with us or in our lives, but until we are ready to admit it, nothing will change. Not only must we admit it, but we must also willingly admit that we cannot fix the condition by ourselves. God has not designed any of us with the level of expertise that allows us to fix every problem and condition we face without the help of someone else. You must have such a desire to fix the condition that you are willing to seek out those whom God has gifted to help you beyond your own limited ability.

Second, when I went to my doctor, he had an idea of what might be wrong, but sent me for x-rays and an MRI in order to be able to see my skeletal frame to determine exactly where and what was causing the problem. You see, often our real issue cannot be labeled or determined by outer manifestations. We have to be able to dig deeper, look deeper and see beyond outer extremities. We can learn how to put on a good look to the extent that no one knows there is a problem. There has to often be some soul searching to determine the root of an issue. After discovering where the problem was, it was then determined that the only way to fix it was through surgery. I had to be cut open in order to be made better. You already get the point, don't you?

Sometimes the road to fixing a condition goes through the city called pain. Some things can't be and won't be fixed without some painful moments. After the surgery and during my period of recovery, several new conditions came up as a result of the surgery. Isn't it amazing how other issues can be discovered when we are "opened up" by a process that is designed to fix something else? You never knew you had a problem in that area until you opened up in another area. After the surgery, and even months into the recovery, I experienced days of pain and crying, sometimes even wishing that I had just left well enough alone. What I did not realize is that some of the pain was evidence that I was healing. You can have days where you wish you had just left things the way they were. The pain in the aftermath can almost seem unbearable, but as I sit here healed, I want you to know that every moment of pain is worth the end result. I would rather be healed than be broken any day of the week.

AY FIVE

LET GOD GIVE YOU HIS PEACE, THEN YOUR DIFFICULTIES WILL NOT DETERMINE YOUR DISPOSITION.

GEM: PRINCIPLES AND PRAGMATISM

I remember very vividly one of my low days after my surgery, which shook me into spiritual reality. I was on the phone with one of my mentors, Dr. Charles Booth, who said to me very succinctly, "Now we will see if you believe what you preach." It reminded me in one sentence what Henri Nouwen postulates in his book, *Physician Heal Thyself.* It is so much easier to talk the principles than it is to walk the principles when we are faced with the reality. I often found myself on some days wondering what I would say to someone who came to me with the same attitude I was portraying. One of my daughters said to me, "if you are the preacher then how can you talk like you don't have any hope when hope is all you preach."

Isn't it so true that we are good at writing down and memorizing scripture after scripture and principle after principle, but seem to get lost somewhere on the bridge that connects the principle with the practice? I was brought to this reality once again as I was reading Matthew's version of the upper room and the Lord's Supper. Jesus said something that I had never thought about because, as it is with so many scriptures that we are familiar with, my familiarity caused me to gloss over what was REALLY said. Jesus broke that bread and notice what Jesus says to them. He said, "Take AND eat." Did you get that? The conjunction "and" means that what Jesus does is give them two different commands that could not be done at the same time. The first thing they were to do was to "take" or "receive" it. However, after receiving it they received a second command to "eat it." The Holy Spirit tapped me on the shoulder and said to me, "that is where so many of you fail." We are willing to receive the bread of life but have trouble eating it in order to live by what we received.

Every Sunday as the Holy Spirit speaks to us through a man or woman of God the riches of the Kingdom, we receive and take the bread, but how many times do we not eat what we take? Beloved, life and blessings are not in the taking of the bread but in the taking and eating of that bread. That is the principle of the great hymn of the church that says, *"Bread of heaven, bread of heaven, FEED ME, 'til I want no more."* To receive it, is principle, but to eat it, is to practice what is preached. I challenge you to do some introspection and see if there is any bread you put on the nightstand and did not digest for your living. Do you really want the blessed life? Then TAKE AND EAT.

AY SIX

SOMETIMES GOD WILL ORCHESTRATE A REJECTION SO THAT YOU ARE AVAILABLE TO BE FOUND.

GEM:
THE PROCESS OF PRODUCING A PROMISE

There are two stories in the Bible that always intrigue me; really the four characters in those two stories: Abraham and Sara; and Elkanah and Hannah. In each case a promise was made about giving birth to a dream at a certain time. What has always intrigued me about those promises is what those characters had to do in order for those promises to come to pass. They could not go to the temple and sow a seed and believe that the seed was going to make it happen. They could not simply and foolishly "name it and claim it" and it would come to pass. They had to participate in the production of the promise. They had to believe in the promise so much so that in spite of what had never happened for them before, they would not give up. They both had physiological odds against them. One lady was old and the other was barren. You could only know you were barren if there had been some attempts to get pregnant that kept failing. This time, a promise is made that what they had been attempting would come to pass. How awesome a faith that they would go back and do again what has never worked before, believing this time that it would work because they had been promised a different result. Get that picture. For the promise to come to fruition, it would take a process of intimate participation.

We live in this new day of fad theology and magic religion that has made for a generation of lazy Christians who want God to be, in the words of Harry Emerson Fosdick, their "cosmic bellhop" who skips down from glory and gives us what we want on a silver platter. I submit to you that living in the power of the Kingdom does not work that way. God leaves room for our participation in bringing about promises. We don't have the luxury of sitting at home and having things dropped in our life. God can do that if He so desires, but God more often than not leaves room for us to activate and exercise our faith by participating in the process of bringing the promise to pass. That production can come in many forms. Only you know what it is you should do to show God your faith in the promise. It could be something as simple as going and filling out the job application. Sowing seeds and having faith are a part of the economy of the Kingdom, but if all you do is sow a seed and then sit at home waiting on the blessing to fall in your lap, you have reduced God to a slot machine. Activate and exercise your faith. Even if you have tried that, whatever that may be, do it again, because this time it comes with a promise that it will happen for you in due season.

$\mathcal{D}$AY SEVEN————————

 YOU NEED PEOPLE IN YOUR LIFE TODAY
WHO ARE COMMITTED TO PROTECTING
YOUR FUTURE.

GEM:

WORSHIP:
An EVENT or an ENCOUNTER

It's eleven o'clock. The praise team opens up. Following
the last song there is a prayer and then a hymn of the
church. After that, there are announcements and a time
to fellowship. After that the choir sings a song, followed
by the giving of tithes and offerings. Then the choir sings
one more song before the Pastor delivers the Word of God
that is hopefully from God. Following that, there is what
is called the "Invitation to Christian discipleship." After
that there is the final blessing and a choral response. You
have just had church, but did you have worship? We have
so mixed and mingled those two words until they don't
seem to have any difference in their definition. Too many
times worship is church; an event to attend when it should
be an encounter that we experience. Events can be

attended without impact, but an encounter always has far reaching impact beyond the moment of the encounter. In an event you can enjoy things, but in an encounter you are transformed.

In the conversion of Saul in Acts chapter nine we see this principle at work. Saul was not alone on that journey of persecution. There were men traveling with him, but as you read the text you will discover that while all of them were at the event and riveted by the event, only one (Saul) got the message. All were at the event but only one had the encounter. I don't know about you, but I would never want to be at an event of spiritual proportion and not have an encounter with God.

Too many times, we come to church and get our "feel good" on, but miss the moment of the Holy Spirit that was supposed to be a moment of encounter. I want to encounter the Divine and be transformed by God's presence in that moment. Don't just come to church. Come seeking an encounter with God that will transform your life and renew your strength. Events don't do that, but encounters can if you let them.

$\mathcal{D}$AY EIGHT

MORNING NUGGET THE DEVIL WANTS TO HOLD YOU IMMOBILE BY THE ROPES OF PAST FAILURES. TODAY MAKE SURE YOU CUT THE ROPE.

GEM:
DENOMINATIONALISM: Theological Necessity or Sociological Convenience

One of the songs I remember from my first pastoral assignment was a song entitled, "In Christ There Is No East or West." The words said, *"In Christ there is no East or West, in Him no South or North, / but one great fellowship of love throughout the whole wide earth."* The premise of those words was that Christ was not divided by geographical regions. Christ does not belong more to one region than another. He isn't worshipped one way in the East and another way in the North. In Christ, there should be ONE GREAT FELLOWSHIP of love. I love to sit and listen to the words of that song, but it brings to my mind a disturbing reality—if Christ is not, cannot and should not be divided, then why do we have so many divisions in the name of the One who has no division? If Christ is one, then why are we separated?

If you were to begin attempting to answer that question, I don't think you will like the answer you come up with. The reality is that most divisions that we name denominations were brought about because of some disagreement on an issue, whether theological or sociological. Someone got upset over infant baptism and a denomination was born. Racism could not be overcome and several denominations were birthed and some stayed in denominations but just started their own version of it, for example, The Southern Baptist Convention. Someone could not handle women in ministry, so another faction came about. Some could not handle the full expression of the life in the Holy Spirit so another faction had to be birthed. It even shows itself in the birth of new churches. Someone got upset and left a church to start another church by the same name with the addition of one word: "Greater" or "First." Oh, if we could ever get our sociology out of our minds and see the Bible as that which should unite us and not divide us, what an awesome pragmatic representation of the Kingdom we would become. If there is no East, West, North or South in Christ then could it be that we have it wrong with the man-made divisions that we have created?

AY NINE

MORNING NUGGET REMEMBER TODAY, YOU ARE NOT RESPONSIBLE FOR PEOPLE, BUT YOU ARE RESPONSIBLE FOR YOUR REACTION TOWARDS THEM.

GEM: BE CALM IN YOUR CHAOS

As I was reading the Bible a few weeks ago, God brought a wonderful revelation to me. When we read the narrative about the creation, we quickly discover that God is a God Who can step out of nowhere and on to nothing and create not just something, but everything. That simple, yet profound truth, helps us to know that if you have nothing, it does not mean that you are unable to be helped. Just look at your own life and see instances of blessings—and how you received those blessings made no sense at the time because to the naked eye, you had nothing going on for you and nothing to offer. What you need to know is that God does His best work with nothing. He made everything when there was nothing. As a matter of fact, God stepped into nothing and then looked around at nothing but chaos and made something heavenly out of nothing. What a compelling thought. God can give you some heaven even if all God has to work with is nothing. That is why every believer ought to make it his or her business to be calm in chaos. Why? Because that is when God begins His best work. You have nothing but bills; nothing but loneliness; nothing but sickness; nothing but confusion in your family—God can step into your nothing, and bring out not only something, but bring out something good. Something good is going to happen to you because God is still God and He does all things good, even if you have nothing but chaos to offer. God stepped into nothing but chaos, fragmentation and disconnection and brought about cosmos, connection and good. God did it then and I am declaring to you that God can do it again.

AY TEN

MORNING NUGGET DON'T LET ANYONE MAKE WITHDRAWALS FROM YOU WHO HAVE MADE NO INVESTMENTS IN YOU.

GEM: HOW BADLY DO YOU REALLY WANT IT?

This story, found at the beginning of the fifth chapter of John, is to me one of the most powerful miracle narratives in all of Holy Writ. Jesus walks into a crowded porch and walks by people who are crippled; passes by people who are blind; ignores people who are lame and all to get to one person. Everyone there has issues but Jesus only speaks to one. Jesus walks by them and goes up to this one man and asks him, "Do you want to be made whole?" The man does not answer. "Do you want to do better?" Instead he gives excuses. He says, "I am not better and it is not my fault. Nobody will help me." I'm not better because of the government. I'm not better because I have a criminal rap sheet. I'm not better because I grew up in poverty. I'm not better because I didn't know my father. I'm not better because the system is not with me. Jesus said, "I didn't ask you who was with you. I'm asking you, do you want a better way of life?"

That is the question today—not what is going on against you, but do you want to have a better life for yourself? God says, forget everything that has happened before now, but right now, do you want your life to be whole? Being whole has nothing to do with having money, cars, relationships, clothes or popularity, but, do you want to stand on your own two feet physically, have it together emotionally, and be on the right path spiritually? That is wholeness. The man gives excuses. Understand that in life there are no such things as excuses, but only choices. You have to make a choice as to whether you will allow yourself to be defined by your difficulty or be an overcomer, by believing that you can make the choice to get up, get out and get on, whether it be physically, mentally or spiritually. There is only one question. The question is not can you have it. It is not why don't you have it. The question is DO YOU WANT IT? Today, make the choice that you are more than your condition wants to tell you that you are and follow the directions to rise and walk.

$\mathcal{D}$AY ELEVEN

MORNING THE WORSE PAIN IN LIFE IS LIVING
NUGGET BEHIND THE WALLS OF UNFORGIVENESS.
BREAK DOWN THE WALL AND MOVE TO
YOUR FUTURE.

GEM:
IT'S NOT YOUR PAST THAT COUNTS

One of my favorite movies is *Soul Food*. One of the great scenes in that movie is when Bird comes home with two friends in the middle of the day and hears noises in the house. She discovers that it is coming from the bathroom and goes and kicks the door open, only to discover her husband, Lem, standing there in nothing but a towel. A fight ensues and Lem ends up telling her that he lost his job because he lied on his application about having a criminal record. He went on to say that he had been on six interviews and no one would hire him because of his record. He had served his time and learned his lesson. He is trying to make his way back into mainstream society. He is married to a good woman and has gotten his life together, but because of a past mistake he is living in a present predicament. His past has authority over his present. While that is a scene from a movie, it is a scene from everyday reality for many people. If you have a record, no matter how hard you have tried to turn your life around, your past will have more say so than your present about your future. If you file for bankruptcy, no matter how well you have done to get back on your feet, it takes seven years to clean it off your record.

Not only does it happen in the system of the world, but it happens in the system of the church. We in the church have this pension and proclivity to gravitate towards holding each other down by constantly speaking about someone's past and the things that they used to do. We treat people as if their worth is only as good as their record. I am glad that God does not operate like the system or like so many people do. The Bible declares He throws our sins into the "sea of forgetfulness." In that sense, if God has forgiven and reconciled my mistakes through the blood of Jesus, then to continue to give them power is to make the resurrection of Christ of no effect. He did not die just to get you and me to heaven. God is not that lonely. Jesus died that we might live for Him on the way to Him. That means that my past is just that...my past. God does not see us by our past. God sees us through the lens of His power, which always gives me promise and potential no matter what my past may be. That means, beloved, that your past nor your current can be an indication of your future potential. Here is some good advice regarding your past: LEAVE IT WHERE YOU LEFT IT. Don't ever forget that your potential speaks to you about your future in spite of your yesterdays.

$\mathcal{D}$AY TWELVE

GEM: DON'T BE YOUR OWN WORSE ENEMY

Let me bring in a little psychology along with some theology. One of the ways that the enemy works on us to keep us in bondage is through tainting our self-worth and self-perception. He seeks to make us think wrong about ourselves so that we will never walk into the fullness of our potential and purpose. What the enemy does is try to make us feel certain ways about ourselves so that we never develop the capacity and the tenacity to reach for anything other than where we are right now. So what happen is, we begin to empower our faults, bad choices, and mistakes to the extent that we begin to believe that whatever that fault, choice or mistake is has enough power to change and downgrade who we really are. Then he brings into our space persons who don't tell us who we really are, but rather, who through what they speak about us, only reinforce what we already feel about ourselves. You see, people and their thoughts and opinions about you are never the issue. The issue is, what do you think about yourself? Whatever people have to say only serves to reinforce what you already believe to be true about yourself. You can't convince me that I am a loser just because you say I am. I already think that I am a loser, and you just validate it for me. You can't make me a failure or convince me that I am a failure just because you say I am. Your saying it only serves to reinforce what I already believe—that I am a failure. If I can begin to think and speak who God says I am, then it will not matter what you say about me or think about me. The fact that I don't believe that about myself will automatically dismiss what you think. Begin to say to yourself, "I AM WHO GOD SAYS I AM, AND I AM WHAT GOD SAYS I CAN BECOME."

$\mathcal{D}$AY THIRTEEN

TODAY, DON'T MAKE A MESS WITH YOUR MOUTH. USE YOUR MOUTH TO SPEAK LIFE AND BLESSINGS.

GEM:
OBEY THE RIDICULOUS AND EXPECT THE MIRACULOUS

There is a wonderful story in the ninth chapter of John's gospel that shows us the lesson of what can happen for us when we are obedient. In this story we find a man who was born without his sight. Jesus spits on the ground and makes clay and then puts the clay over the man's eyes.

In that day and time one of the medical solutions that was often used was spit and mud. Jesus begins the miracle by working with the medicine of that day. (So much for those who want to dismiss medicine as a tool to be used by God.) Jesus puts the spittled mud in the man's eyes and nothing changes. The man still couldn't see. He received the ministry of the Lord but still couldn't see. You can receive the touch of the Master and things can still look muddy. Let me give you this word of encouragement: Don't be discouraged by the mud. If you're willing to look muddy for a while it will pay off.

Here is my question? Can you praise Him while you have mud on your face and no change yet in your life? The devil hates muddy worshippers, because he knows he has no power to mess with them because they have nothing for him to mess with. Everything for them is muddy and feels muddy. Have you ever found yourself at that junction of life? As you continue to read the story something should jump out at you. Things don't get clear until the next step is taken. While things are muddy, Jesus then tells the man to go and wash in the pool of Siloam. The man follows some crazy instructions. The spit and mud did not give the man his sight, but now Jesus wants him to go wash in a pool, and the man does it. I want you to notice the text. It says that the man **came back seeing**. In other words he did not get the result of the miracle until after he had done the ridiculous thing he was told to do.

I declare to you that things will stay muddy until you take the next step of obedience. You've got to be obedient, even if it makes you look ridiculous. Your blessing is in your obedience. Do whatever it takes, no matter what it takes. If I am willing to do the ridiculous, He will be willing to perform the miraculous.

$\mathcal{D}$AY FOURTEEN

MORNING NUGGET PEOPLE MISTREATING YOU DOESN'T GIVE YOU THE RIGHT TO MISTREAT THEM. AS CHRISTIANS, WE LIVE UNDER A DIFFERENT ETHIC.

GEM:
LEARN TO PLEASE GOD

One of the great challenges of the Christian faith is learning to live this life without the necessity of signs in order for one to move forward. One of the reasons that I think the writer of the book of Hebrews says to us that it is impossible to please God without faith is because when we exercise our faith we show that we have such a naked trust in God for our lives that we won't let what things look like around us become what moves and motivates us. It pleases God when He can see that no matter what things may look like, you still will stick with Him. It pleases God to see you walking through a situation that ought to make you quit believing that He is still in control. After all, anybody can trust God when things are going the way they want them to go. But can you still trust God when everything around you is contradictory to how you want to believe things are going to turn out? Can you be faithful when all you have is revelation? You see, the only people who need signs are people who don't have faith, because when you have faith, hearing is enough. When God makes a promise, God does not give immediate evidence because evidence is what you don't need when you have faith. Faith is the evidence of things NOT seen. Some people think that you are crazy because they see you walking around with your head held up and they know you have not received a word of confirmation. It is holy confidence that if God tells me something, it has to come to pass. If you can believe God for something that He told you when He did not show you anything, that is when God is pleased. What pleases God more than your praise and more than your going to church, is your ability to trust Him when you cannot trace Him. Make the decision today that what you want as your aim and priority is to please God.

$\mathcal{D}$AY FIFTEEN

REMEMBER BEING A CHRISTIAN WILL GIVE YOU OCCASIONS TO BE OFFENDED. HANDLE IT RIGHT AND GOD WILL GET THE GLORY.

GEM:
GOD IS AFTER SOMETHING

I vividly remember once going up to my son, Joshua's room to find him something to wear for church. Much to his delight and my chagrin, every suit in his closet no longer fit him. He had outgrown every suit I could put my hand on. He was in heaven because he hates wearing suits! As I looked deeper into the closet, I discovered two suits with tags still on them. I called down to my wife to inquire about the suits. She proceeded to explain to me that she had purchased them a year ago but they were too big for him at the time. She did not return them because they did not have one in the size he was at that time. She then said something that has stuck with me every since that day. She said she put it in the closet knowing it was too big for him then, but knew that he would eventually grow to fit into them.

What a powerful illustration of the desire of God for all of our lives. He has blessings waiting for all of us that require development before we can be clothed in them. God will never risk His glory on someone who is not developed enough to wear what He has for them. God is not after your desires. God is not after your delight. He is after your development.

Now, development can be a tricky thing because some things come along with it that you may not necessarily like. You cannot walk into a wealthy place without first going through some things. You will not walk into purpose without going through some pain. And I just want to tell somebody that whatever you do, don't curse the part you don't like because your best self will be developed in those rough places. The old folk used to sing this song: *Tell me how did you feel when you come out the wilderness...Leaning on the Lord.* The implication was that before I went in the wilderness I may have been leaning on myself. But where did I learn how to lean and depend on the Lord? In the wilderness. Can I tell you the other verses? *I felt like running...I felt like singing...I felt like clapping.* Every now and then you need to take a little time and thank God for the wilderness. That is why the devil can't stand you— not just because you came out, but because of how you came out. You came out having allowed the wilderness to be used by God to further develop you. God is after developing you. Don't miss out on wearing something God is holding in the closet with your name on it. Let Him help you grow up so you can wear it proudly.

$\mathcal{D}$AY SIXTEEN

MORNING NUGGET WHEN YOU ALLOW OTHERS TO STIMULATE YOUR ACTIONS THEN YOU BECOME A SLAVE TO THEIR CONCEPTS. SLAVERY ENDED LONG AGO!

GEM:
SHOW ME YOUR FRIENDS AND I WILL SHOW YOU YOUR FUTURE

There is an old saying that goes like this: "If you show me your friends, then I will tell you your future." It speaks to the power and impact of the people that you hang around. Make no mistake about it, the crowd you hang with makes a difference in the decisions that you make concerning your life. We see it over and over in the Bible. We see the prodigal son get turned out by going to a far country and hooking up with people whose norm for living goes against who he is as a Jew. We also see this in Peter and his denial, when he was found warming himself "around the fire" with those who were not on the side of the Lord, and this led him to become comfortable enough to deny Jesus, because in that crowd that would not be strange.

The crowd that we travel with can make a difference in our lives. If the crowd that we associate with is supportive of our efforts to do the right thing, then their support can be what leads us to the right decision. Let's be honest. It's not always easy to do the right thing without a push from somebody else. As a matter of fact, if you look around at the crowd that you hang out with it will tell you something about yourself. I heard somebody say one day that water has a way of seeking its own level. In other words, the water will sink to the level of everything else around it. Losers hang out with losers. Drunks hang out with drunks. Gossipers hang out with gossipers. Small-minded people hang out with other small-minded people.

Anybody in your circle who tries to speak against your happiness and against your liberty is someone you need to get rid of right now, because it is obvious that they need you to be miserable, and need you to need them for them to feel needed. Relationships are important to your future. You should be so determined to reach the destiny determined for you by God that you will dismiss people who can't help you get there. Use discernment to determine who belongs in your space. Be bold enough to walk away from people who can't help you evolve into the person God designed you to be and the destiny God created you to walk in. These people will not always be evil people. Sometimes it may be persons whose purpose in your life has been accomplished and their season is over. Sometimes it may be good people who just don't have an assignment in your life right now. That is why it takes discernment, because everyone you need to distance yourself from may not be evil. Begin today praying for that spirit of discernment so that you can, by your friends, say something positive about your future.

$\mathcal{D}$AY SEVENTEEN

REMEMBER, PEOPLE WILL ALWAYS TRY TO REDUCE YOU IN ORDER TO MANAGE YOU. YOU ALREADY HAVE A MANAGER— GOD.

GEM:
A GOOD THING OR A GOD THING

Anyone who is in any type of management will tell you that one of, if not the most important concept in management theory is, the concept of vision. Effective leadership requires vision. When you do not have vision you have no idea where you are headed. Vision sets the course and determines the destination. Although we hear more about it today in this modern society, the reality is that vision is not a new concept. If you were to travel back in antiquity, you will discover that Solomon told us that when you do not have vision you are on your way to perishing.

What is vision? Some would say that vision is a hopeful image for the future. Someone else has said that it is a standard for performance that provides direction for the collective and unified effort. It permits you to see a future that is more desirable than the present. Vision concentrates on the future. It is prospective and not retrospective. It is about seeing what is ahead and not dwelling on the past. It does not see things as they are and ask why? But vision sees things that never were and asks why not? Vision is seeing what your eyes can't see or mind can't comprehend, because most of the time it is not based on facts. If it were based on favorable facts, you run the risk of giving the situation or yourself credit for it when it comes to pass.

You remember Noah, don't you? God tells Noah to build an ark in the middle of a desert. He gives Noah the vision of building an ark for His own purpose and plan. It does not rain in the desert. He was nowhere near a body of water, but God said to build the boat and tell your family to get on it. I know you don't understand it but build it anyway. You know it is vision when God requires something of you that you do not understand. Vision is needed in the church. Vision is needed for your business. Vision is even needed for how you will perform your job. You need vision for your own life. You need something that makes you get out of bed everyday. You need something that gives you hope for your future. And your vision needs to line up with the vision God has for you.

Every good thing is not vision. Sometimes it is the result of human desires. Just because it is a desire does not mean it is Divine design. Yes, the Word says that God will give you the desires of your heart, but please do not damage the meaning by pulling it out of context and without proper theological understanding. I must first submit myself and my ways to the ways of God. It is at that point that my desires will begin to line up with God's design for my life and result in my only desiring the things that go along with His design. Seek out the vision of God. It may be more difficult to bring it to pass than a good thing, but you will be blessed.

$\mathcal{D}$AY EIGHTEEN———————

GEM:
REDEFINING RELATIONSHIPS

I must give credit where credit is due. The title of this particular devotional entry came from a sermon of this very title preached by my late homiletics mentor, Dr. Miles Jerome Jones. I use it in memory of Him.

I am absolutely convinced that next to money, the one area in which the enemy causes the most damage in the lives of believers is in the area of relationships. Many people are in the state they are in emotionally, physically and even spiritually because of what I call "relationship mismanagement." If we are honest with ourselves, we would have to admit that most of us at some point in our lives have been the victim of the hurts, pains and lessons of relationship mismanagement. Some of the hookups we have experienced have caused us great consternation, pain and misery. When I read the story of the creation of

Adam and Eve, I am reminded of the importance of proper relationships in our lives and God's desire to place proper people in our lives. For many of us the challenge is to change the culture of connections we allow and redefine relationships by the standards of the Almighty. God is concerned about our relationships. He is concerned about who we hang out with and who we hookup with. When you read the second chapter of Genesis, you will discover that God is greatly concerned about us having right relationships. Have you ever thought that even though Adam had company, God still declared him to be alone? He had God and he had the animals, but he was still alone.

God wants to rectify loneliness in your life. You can have people all around you, but not have good company. God wants to deal with the feeling of loneliness because people who are lonely manifest their loneliness in destructive ways. You go from relationship to relationship because you are trying to fill the void that you feel. You are on the down low with persons who you know are not for you simply because you are trying to deal with your loneliness. You swore you were through with them, but you keep going right back to them because you are lonely. You know he is not Mr. Right, but at least he is Mr. Right Now, because you are lonely. Or maybe it's friendships with people that you know add nothing of benefit to your life. You let them in your space. Could it be that the reason they gravitate to you and you gravitate to them is because misery loves company? God wants to hook you up with some good company—People who can bless your life; People who can bring fulfillment to your life; People who can add something spiritual to your life. That just may mean you need to start redefining relationships, not by your wants but by Godly standards.

DAY NINETEEN

GEM:
WHEN WAS THE LAST TIME YOU VOIDED?

That was the question I was asked by a nurse as I was getting ready for a procedure on my right vocal chord in order to augment it because it had been paralyzed through an earlier surgical procedure. Now I am quite sure that you know what she meant in that medical context (If you don't, it means when was the last time I went to the restroom). As she mentioned it though, my mind, even as I lay there awaiting this surgery, went spiritual concerning the idea of voids.

A void is when something is missing. It is when you get rid of something or when something is released. I saw this at work in the life of Saul as he was on his way to becoming the king. The story of Saul is one that we only know pieces of. We know that he was the king prior to

David. We know that he lost his anointing and tried to go gangster on David and tried to take David out. Besides that, we don't know much about Saul. The truth of the matter is we know more about the ending of his life than we do about the beginning of his life. We know much more about his kingship after he had been fired but left in the position. What an awful thought...to be in the position, but with no power.

We don't know much about him in the position before David comes on the scene. I found very interesting the beginning of the story of the life of Saul as the anointed one. Come with me, today, back to the beginning of the journey to kingship that is laid out for us in the ninth chapter of First Samuel. As I was looking at the beginning of the life of Saul, I saw something powerful in what God was doing to get Saul on the road to his destiny. God was ready to put Saul on the road to purpose and destiny and this chapter begins the awakening of Saul to what God had for him. Here is what I saw: Some of Saul's father's donkeys came up missing, and he sent Saul looking for them. During that time and in that culture, donkeys were used to transact business and transport cargo. Saul's father could not do business as usual because something was missing. There was a void created or allowed by God that became what propelled Saul into his new assignment as king.

God will sometimes orchestrate a void in your life because we never seek the things of God as long as things are going smoothly for us. Sometimes God has to allow a void in some area of your life because when you have everything you think you need you will go with business as usual. If you had not felt like something was missing you may not have ever left the house and gone looking. God just allowed the donkeys to get lost to give Saul a reason to get out of the house and go searching for something better that he never would have found if the donkeys had not gone missing. God let the donkeys go missing so Saul would go find what God had for Him in the first place. Maybe the void that you are feeling is not a void you need to be filling. Maybe it is the very void you are dealing with that God wants to use to start you on the journey to a new assignment. Instead of asking God to help you find the donkeys you should be asking God to show you the destiny. I don't know who this is for...but what you lost is no comparison to what you are going to find! Have you voided lately? Maybe it's that time.

AY TWENTY

MORNING NUGGET REMEMBER...GOD'S PRIMARY PURPOSE IS NOT TO MAKE YOU HAPPY BUT TO MAKE YOU HOLY, AND BEING HOLY WILL MAKE YOU HAPPY.

GEM: TRUST IN THE CONSISTENCY OF GOD'S CHARACTER NO MATTER HOW CONTRADICTORY YOUR CONTEXT

Genesis Chapter 17

This chapter in the life of Abraham begins one of the more powerful stories of the Old Testament on the faith of a saint and the power of the promises of Yahweh. God, in this chapter, makes a promise to Abraham that God was going to give him an heir, and that he would produce this heir, even at his age. Abraham was having a little trouble believing in it because of his current condition. What God does in verse seven is a beautiful picture of the love of God and God's commitment to His word and promise. He says something to Abraham almost in anticipation of what Abraham is going to say in verse eight. He almost tries to beat Abraham to the punch and save him from allowing the doubts that are in his head to come out of his mouth.

Abraham is old. Sarah is old. The context just does not match the promise. God then, in verse seven, makes a wonderful statement that all would do good to remember when life does not seem to line up with what God has for you or is telling you. What God is telling Abraham is look where I brought you from already and how I blessed you and gave you the wealth of five kings in one day. I got you to where you are faster than you should have gotten there. You may not be where you want to be, but God got you to where you are faster than you would have gotten there on your own. You weren't supposed to have what you have as quick as you have. The Lord is saying, I did it for you. Now Abraham in this moment when you start to have doubts because of your age or because of your wife's age, remember what I can do quicker than expected because I have already done it for you. And Abraham, I am the same God today that I was when I did it for you then. In other words, don't try God by your current context, but trust God based on holy history.

Your context may be contradicting your promise, but just remember that God, Yahweh, the GREAT I AM is always consistent. The next time you start to think that you are running out of time, just remember God. Remember your holy history and make it bigger than your current condition. The next time you feel like you are out of time and that your life is not lining up as you think it should, just remember what God has already done for you. Don't allow your problems to overrule your promise. I know what it looks like. I know it's getting late in the game, but just remember who God is.

$\mathcal{D}$AY TWENTY-ONE

GOD CAN TAKE WHAT SATAN SENDS TO DESTROY YOU AND USE IT TO DEVELOP YOU. REMEMBER, DIFFICULTY IS A PART OF YOUR DEVELOPMENT.

GEM: STOPPING SHORT AND MISSING OUT

Did you know that the blessed place Abraham was promised he would walk into was given to him almost by default? Now that I have your attention, read the end of Genesis chapter eleven, beginning in verse thirty-one. When you read it, you will discover that his father, Terah, was on his way to Canaan, but he messed up. He should have walked into what Abraham is about to walk into. Well, what happened? HE SETTLED TOO SOON and took good when better was available. If you take your Bible and go back to chapter eleven, you will see that Terah died in Haran, beneath where he should have been because he settled. It says that he took his family out of Ur to go to Canaan, but got to Haran and settled there. He grew comfortable living short of Canaan. He was comfortable in Haran. Now, Haran was said to be a metropolitan city. It was an aristocratic place, so it stands to reason that when Terah saw the richness of Haran over against having no clue of what he would find in Canaan, he decided to stop right there. Haran had the look. It looked like the place to be. It was a good place. It looked like the best place to be, but best is not described by what you might get. Best is described by being in the place God destined you to be and settling for nothing less. You can be in a good place without it being a God place. Terah gets more stuff but settles for less of God. From appearance it looks like he has God because of where he settles.

You can spend all of your time going after stuff and miss God. Your blessing is not in your stuff, but your blessing is in your obedience to God. And if you are not careful you can stop short and miss God. In this day of prosperity preaching and materialistic theology, we need to understand clearly that having things doesn't always give you God or God's blessings. I would rather know I am in the place where God assigns me than be in a place that gives me "the look" of being prosperous. Don't settle for things that look good. Don't settle too soon. The text says that when you stop short of where God desires you to be, you will stop short and miss out. Look around at your life today and ask yourself this critical question: Is it good or is it God?

DAY TWENTY-TWO

STAY IN TOUCH WITH YOUR LIMITATIONS SO THAT YOU STAY IN TOUCH WITH GOD WHO HAS NO LIMITS.

GEM:
A CHANGE IN ENVIRONMENT

Come back with me to the continuation of the text and story we began looking at on yesterday. In the next chapter, God now comes to Abraham and shares with him the wonderful promise and blessing He is going to make out of him and give to him. Have you ever noticed that before God gives the promise He first gives out some instructions? Obedience is always the key to the blessed life. We love to sing, "when the praises go up the blessings come down," but as my father has often said, "everything that's cute is not correct." You don't get blessed just because you shout. You get blessed because you know how to be obedient and faithfully follow what God has instructed.

The first thing God tells Abraham to obey is change his environment. God says, "Abraham get out of your country from your daddy's house." We discovered on yesterday that it was his daddy's house that wanted to settle. Leave all of the people who want to stay settled. The implication is right in the text in the words, YOUR DADDY'S HOUSE. They think like his daddy thought. You will never take possession if you have people in your space who are scared to take risks. As long as you surround yourself with people who will settle for what is comfortable, you will not make it to the place God has assigned you to be in. If you have people around you who push you to stay settled in the comfortable, then LEAVE. Some people in your space can't see it and will speak against it, because they like where they are and want you to stay there with them. They have been together all of this time, but God steps in and says I know you have been with them all of this time but now it is time for separation.

Isn't it interesting that God's call for separation comes at the start of a new chapter? This is the beginning of chapter twelve. As you begin to change your environment, know that some people who have been with you are not assigned to go with you to the next chapter of your life. Don't make the mistake of making someone permanent who was intended to be transitional. There are some people who are assigned to go with you for only part of the journey, and not the whole journey, and you need to know when their time is up. You need to say to them, DON'T TRY TO HOLD ME BACK JUST BECAUSE YOU CAN'T GO WITH ME. I would rather be alone with God than be with a bunch of people who are willing to settle. Lord, help me to do an inventory of my environment, and as I enter my new chapter, help me to leave "last chapter people" behind who do not belong with me in my next chapter.

*D*AY TWENTY-THREE

MORNING NUGGET IF YOU DON'T KNOW WHO YOU ARE OTHERS WILL TRY TO TELL YOU WHO YOU ARE. WHO ARE YOU?

GEM: **READ THE FINE PRINT**

I can remember once getting sick upon taking a certain medicine. I had been told that this was the best over-the-counter medication for what I was dealing with. I could not understand why it had made me so sick, until I picked the bottle up and read beyond the instructions and saw more of the fine print. In the fine print were warnings of what to expect if you took this medicine. There were certain things that came with taking this medication that should have prohibited me from taking it, but because I did not read the fine print to see what all came with this medicine I ended up making myself sick.

As I look out into the church world today, it becomes obvious to me that the brand of Kingdom we are "pushing" has forgotten about the fine print that tells us what comes with walking this way. The new prosperity movement is suggesting that the material gain you have becomes the barometer to measure the favor of God on your life and the sign that you are "living right with God." As a result, now people spend all of their time trying to get rich and trying to accumulate things so that they can "prove" their faith in God and God's favor with them. If being rich is the evidence of being saved then a whole lot of us are on our way to hell. If having things is the measuring stick for how deep your faith is then a lot of us are living in shallow waters. If living a life of perfection is the evidence of the flow of the Spirit in your life, then a whole lot of us are without the Spirit. So as a consequence, we have people running around trying to figure out how to be rich. Until they reach those heights, they beat themselves up as not being spiritual enough. The problem with this theology is it goes against the grain of everything that is seen in the Word of God—the fine print. May I give you the fine print of this medicine called Christianity and salvation? Jesus said:

"Foxes have holes, and birds of the air have nests; but the Son of man hath not where to lay his head."

This verse shows that if you are going to walk with Him, there will be seasons where you may not have anywhere to lay your head. Jesus also said that in this life you are going to have tribulations. Those tribulations can come in a variety of shapes and sizes. They can be financial. They can be physical. They can be vocational. They can be relational. The fine print says that it goes with the territory. Whatever you do, read and understand the fine print so that you don't make yourself sick because you didn't know what to expect.

The difference in this spiritual application and my earthly reality was the fine print of the medicine bottle should have kept me from taking it. In the Christian life however, the fine print lets you know what to expect as you take each dose, but take it nonetheless, because the struggle is a part of what gets you to the prize. Digest it all, because in spite of the challenges of the fine print, what you receive in the end are blessings beyond measure. Jesus did not end by saying you will have tribulation. He ended with a word of assurance—*"be of good cheer, I have overcome the world."* This medicine is good for the soul.

$\mathcal{D}$AY TWENTY-FOUR

MORNING NUGGET WHEN YOU HAVE NO CONVICTIONS YOU HAVE NO CAUSE. WHEN YOU HAVE NO CAUSE YOU ARE JUST A CONVERSATION.

GEM:
NO 'GET OUT OF JAIL FREE' CARD

Two of the great tools of the Kingdom that we sometimes misuse are the instruments of praise and prayer. Neither prayer nor praise were given to us as tools to help us get out of things that we don't like. When rightly understood, prayer and praise are tools to help us with our endurance than they are to grant us deliverance.

One place where this can be seen very succinctly is in that great narrative in the book of Acts chapter sixteen where Paul and Silas find themselves in jail as a result of messing up a man's hustle. It is my humble opinion that we have done a great disservice to this text and as a result come to the wrong conclusion about their prayer and praise service. The text says, "At midnight they were singing and praying." We have interpreted that to mean that they started doing it when things got the darkest— at midnight. But that is not what the text says. The word "at" implies that when midnight came they were already in praise and prayer. They were not doing it because things had gotten worse. When things got worse they continued doing it. That is why midnight didn't bother them. They already had their focus on God. They were not doing this as a get-out-of-trouble weapon. They were doing it even before things got worse.

When worship is your way of life, you don't just do it when trouble comes, in an effort to get out of the trouble. When worship is your way of life, when you are a worshipper and a real prayer warrior, trouble doesn't have the impact on you that it could have.

The text says they were doing it TO GOD. In other words, their words were not about their situation but about their Savior. They weren't talking about what they were going through. They were talking about the God Who could bring them through. You see, when you put your mind on God and remind yourself who God is, it will remind you that whatever you are going through is not so big that God can't solve it or keep you while you are in it. You have to learn to bless God even when the prayer is not answered yet. You have to learn to lift God up even when you don't know how things are going to turn out. Paul and Silas were not doing it because of what they were in. They were doing it because it was just who they were. You may be asking, well, how do you know? I can prove it. Verse sixteen is the key. They were on the way to the place of prayer when all of this started. It was time for worship when their intentions seemed to be interrupted and sidetracked. I believe that even though they were not in the place they were going to, they still could participate in the purpose they were going to do in that place. The place becomes wherever you find yourself. You make where you are the altar of prayer and worship. Nothing can interrupt it. Nothing can stop it. If this is what we intended to do, then we will do it no matter where we have to do it.

Challenge yourself to become a worshipper and a prayer warrior, not because you need something or need to get out of a bad situation, but because it's who you are. I guarantee you, if it does not get you deliverance it will get you endurance. God will be moved to do something on your behalf—either take you out of it or keep you while you go through it.

$\mathscr{D}$AY TWENTY-FIVE

YOU WILL NEVER GET AHEAD CARRYING OLD STUFF. DIVEST SO YOU CAN INVEST.

GEM: "A WORTHY WALK"

It has been said by medical authorities that walking is one of the best forms of exercise. Walking stimulates the heart and the lungs. It increases the blood flow throughout the body and can help to bring about weight loss. It has been said that in many cities people are being encouraged to leave their automobiles in their garage and begin walking. I once saw a commercial that said, "WALKING MAKES THE GOOD LIFE BETTER." Did you know that the average person takes 7,000 to 8,000 steps a day and about two and one-half billion steps a year? That means that in your lifetime, you will walk approximately 115,000 miles. There is something about being a walker that comes with unprecedented benefits. We see this principle of walking being beneficial at work long before the exercise craze ever came along.

Look with me at a gentleman by the name of Enoch. He is one of two men who lived on this earth and went to Heaven without passing through the portals of death. Next to Jesus, he is the only one of whom it was written that he "pleased God." Because of the way that he lived, he is lifted up to us as a hero of the faith. The Bible sums up Enoch's life of faith with four words: "Enoch walked with God." There is not much else known about him. He was not nobility. He was not a warrior. He was not a statesman or a scientist. He didn't accomplish anything remarkable by the standards of society. He was not like Daniel. He was not like David. He was not like Joseph, Moses or Abraham. The only thing we are told about him is that he walked with God. He found a way to stay holy in a hellish world.

Notice, if you will, that Enoch walked **with** God and not **for** God. Many want to walk for God, but not with God. Enoch walked WITH God. That means where God went, he went WITH God. God was his guide. I am sure embedded in that is the reality that Enoch went some places where he didn't want to be and did some things that he didn't want to do because he walked with God.

Please do not miss the order of the wording for it is filled with intentionality concerning the way of walking. God did not walk with Enoch. Enoch was not the one giving out the daily itinerary and God following his direction. No. Enoch walked with God. What a blessing to have God as your walking partner and your guide. When you walk with God you know that nothing or nobody can separate you or defeat you. When you are walking with God, it becomes a privilege and an honor. The words of that great hymn of the church come to my mind. *"Lead me, guide me along the way / For if you lead me I will not stray / Lord let me walk each day <u>WITH THEE</u> / Lead me, oh Lord, lead me."*

DAY TWENTY-SIX

MORNING NUGGET REMEMBER...WHAT PEOPLE CALL YOU DOES NOT CHANGE WHO YOU ARE. GOD DECIDED WHO YOU ARE LONG BEFORE THEY CAME ALONG.

GEM:
ALL YOU HAVE TO DO IS ASK

I start this devotion by making a statement that will shock many of you because it goes against everything that we have been taught and heard most of our lives. That is this: it's all right to question God. I know many right now are shaking their heads because we have all been told at some point or another to never question God. But I want to submit to you that God does not have a problem with it. It's all right, first, because God already knows everything, which means He knows about our questions before we ask them. Not asking doesn't mean the questions are not there. It only means that we are covering them behind some religious façade.

Second, it's all right to question God because there is a

difference in questioning God and doubting God. Sometimes we confuse the two. To doubt means that I say, I'm not sure if I believe. To question means that while I believe, I just don't understand.

Third, it's all right, because sometimes you only learn by asking questions.

Fourth, it's all right, because God can handle our questions. God is not fragile. If God can handle our sins, then I know He can handle our questions. If God can handle our faults, then I know God can handle our questions. God is not some fragile person who falls apart and is easily offended and insulted.

Fifth, it's all right, because some of the strongest personalities in the Bible did it. Abraham laughed and fell on his face at the thought of being a daddy and asked a question of God, "Can a man at my age give birth to a child?" Moses on the backside of Mount Horeb while in a conversation with God asked of God, "Who am I that I should go?" Job in the midst of sitting on an ash heap having no reason for his condition asked over and over, "Why?" John the Baptist, who found himself in a prison cell facing death sent a question to Jesus, "Are you the Christ or should we look for somebody else?" Even Jesus hanging on the cross of Calvary found Himself lifting a question heavenward, "Why have you forsaken Me?"

There will be moments when your condition does not line up with your claim, and you find yourself looking for answers. Know in those times that God can handle your question. In our heart of hearts, there are moments when we have questions, disappointments, difficulties and sometimes anger at the ways of God. Just know this, after you ask the question, God is not obligated to answer, but we are obligated to trust Him.

$\mathcal{D}$AY TWENTY-SEVEN ————

A PIECE OF ADVICE: WHILE YOU WAIT ON THE MOVE OF GOD, WORSHIP WHILE YOU WAIT. IT WILL SHOW GOD THAT IT'S NOT ABOUT WHAT YOU'RE WAITING ON.

GEM: HAVE YOU GOT GOOD RELIGION?

One of the songs I vividly remember singing, as a kid while growing up in the Bethel church was a song entitled, "Have You Got Good Religion?" The song was in the call and response motif, as most things are in the Black church. The leader would sing to you, "Have you got good religion?" and the response was, "Certainly Lord." The jist of the song was whether or not you had a clear understanding of God and what He has done for you. For our ancestors, the term religion was not about church or style or denomination. For them, religion was your belief system. It was what you thought about God. To make it through the vicissitudes that come in this life, that is what you need—good religion. In the language of scholarship we would call it good theology. The most powerful tool you have at your disposal when it comes to making decisions and moving forward in life is what you think about God. What you believe about God can shape your thoughts, your dreams, your goals, and your desires. When you have a good sense of who God is and what God is able to do, it will help you redefine everything about your life. It happened with and for Mary during the discussion about her being the human instrumentality to bring into this world the Christ. She tells this ethereal emissary from Eternity named Gabriel that this is not possible because she is a virgin. Her current condition does not allow for this possibility in her eyes. When Mary brings this point up, it is the phrase about God that becomes the crux of the matter. The angel said to Mary, understand that God doing this in your life has nothing to do with you and everything to do with God. WITH GOD NOTHING IS IMPOSSIBLE. There's nothing that God can't do. When you believe that, it can give you an assurance beyond anything you can imagine. WITH GOD NOTHING IS IMPOSSIBLE. In other words, God keeps His promises no matter how difficult the circumstances may seem. However, here is the catch: It is not just enough to say that; It's not even enough to just believe that. You then have to accept it and submit to it. I know a lot of people who can hear the truth but not allow the truth that they hear to come to power in their lives. The key to the blessing is not in what Gabriel said as much as it was in what Mary followed up with. She accepted what she heard about God as truth and submitted to what she accepted. What Mary was really saying was: IT'S POSSIBLE. That's all I want to say to encourage someone reading this. IT'S POSSIBLE. I don't know what it is you have been believing God for and maybe the enemy has you about convinced that it can't happen for you, but...IT'S POSSIBLE. That job that you have been holding out for and have almost given up on...IT'S POSSIBLE. That business you thought would have started by now and now you are ready to throw in the towel...IT'S POSSIBLE. The healing to your body that doctors say can't happen for you...IT'S POSSIBLE. Those bills you were convinced would keep you from starting over because you always have more month than you do money...IT'S POSSIBLE. Have you got good religion? Certainly Lord, because I know that with You it is possible.

$\mathcal{D}$AY TWENTY-EIGHT

MORNING NUGGET WHAT YOU THINK ABOUT YOU CAN BRING ABOUT. I WONDER WHAT YOU'RE THINKING, TODAY. DWELL ON THE RIGHT THOUGHTS AND GET THE RIGHT BLESSINGS.

GEM:
FROM PAIN TO PRAISE

When one reads the Psalms of David you will quickly discover that David had highs and lows. As a matter of fact, he had high highs and very low lows. One minute he is a great man of faith extolling the wonderful works of God and the next minute we see him begging God to get him out of trouble. It happens once again here in Psalm 69. In the Psalm that we study today we see David in a prayer of desperation. When you read the Psalm you will discover that he has crushing challenges all around him. In verse four he starts to talk about the reason for his situation. David is feeling the mental and emotional weight of the haters and their plots to get him. He is crying out to God to help him and to rescue him. He cries out to God to vindicate him against their accusations.

He cries out to God to deliver him from the traps that the enemy has laid. He says in verse four that he had to restore something that was not even his fault. He had to repay something he had not stolen. David says that he is sick. He has no friends. He has no comforters. What a place to be in. He is the anointed one but here he is in a mess and admitting it. Have you ever cried out to God when you had taken all you could take? What do you do when your life is at that point? After you have prayed every prayer, worshipped and quoted the Word and things still aren't better, how should you respond when you have done all of that and nothing around you seems to change? In verse thirty, after everything David has been through, after letting out all of his emotions, he says I will offer praise to God. It's called the sacrifice of praise. It's a sacrifice to say, THANK YOU, JESUS, when nothing has changed. It's a sacrifice to say PRAISE THE LORD! when you can barely say anything at all. It's a sacrifice to say GLORY TO GOD! when it seems as if you have lost more than you have gained. That kind of praise comes at a price. You would rather be quiet. You would prefer to complain. You would rather continue to talk about your mistreatment at the hands of others. You would prefer to throw your pity party over your sickness. But you have been doing that and it has gotten you nowhere. Now it's time to give Him the praise. When you don't feel like it; when you aren't even sure of yourself anymore; when you feel like you are about to go under; when you know that the battle is far from over—that's when you offer up the sacrifice of praise. When I have to restore what I did not steal, I will offer up the sacrifice of praise. When I have been falsely accused, instead of answering insult for insult, I will offer the sacrifice of praise.

When people misunderstand you, offer up the sacrifice of praise. When friends take out their frustrations on you, offer up the sacrifice of praise. When you are given a medical report that is not good, offer up the sacrifice of praise. When you have lost your job, offer up the sacrifice of praise. When tears are running down your cheek, offer up the sacrifice of praise. I dare you to give God the sacrifice of praise. You give Him the praise and in exchange God will give you peace.

$\mathscr{D}$AY TWENTY-NINE

MORNING NUGGET YOU WILL NEVER HAVE VICTORY IF YOU PLAY THE VICTIM. DON'T EXERCISE THE RIGHT TO FAIL JUST BECAUSE YOU HAVE SOMEONE TO PLACE THE BLAME ON. SUCCEED IN SPITE OF THEM.

GEM: DON'T BE AFRAID OF THE DARK

The battle between God and Satan, speaking from a point of imagery, has always been one between light and darkness. When Satan attempted to commit cosmic mutiny and take over heaven and God in righteous indignation had to kick him out, the prophet Isaiah says to us that it was like seeing a falling star. Satan then became the ruler of darkness. Jesus on an occasion called Himself the Light of the world. Jesus then goes on to say about those who follow Him that YOU ARE THE LIGHT OF THE WORLD. In other words, wherever there is darkness, when you show up you ought to change the substance of the environment.

Many of us growing up did not like the dark. If we were to be honest, many of us still don't like the dark. There is something seemingly sinister about it. It is hard to move around in the dark. You often cannot see objects that are in your way as you walk in the dark. I submit to you however, that it is in the dark where God determines the level of our trust in Him.

We are called to constantly seek the Lord. That means that our context or condition does not cancel out that mandate. Even when my life is in a dark place I am called to seek God. Many times God only moves a situation when it is dark and you are looking for Him. God will move things when you look for Him. I don't want you to miss what I am saying. If you seek the Lord, not to get you out, but just seeking the Lord in your dark hours, God will start to move things on your behalf. If you learn how to worship God when it's dark, seeking God's face and not His hand, you will look up and God will have moved some things, some situations, some people, and some difficulties out of your way, just because you didn't quit, but kept on seeking Him.

Some people can only seek Him when things are light, but real worshippers know how to seek Him even when it is dark. Sometimes God wants to see if you will praise Him in the dark like you expect the lights to come back on. That's the kind of praise and worship that will drive the devil crazy. He is the prince of darkness, which means he stakes some claim to dark territory and yet you have the nerve to worship God in territory that the enemy thinks is his. Somebody can say I am in a dark situation right now, but I have enough nerve to seek God no matter what I am going through.

Child of God, don't be afraid of the dark. God is there. He is active even if He seems absent. God is there in your darkest hours. God is omnipresent, which means there is no place where God's presence is not. If you seek God, then that presence will be made manifest to you even in the dark. Remember, God is there, so "seek ye the Lord while He may be found."

$\mathcal{D}$AY THIRTY

 **MORNING NUGGET** TODAY, CHANGE THE WAY YOU PRAY. DON'T PRAY FOR WHAT YOU NEED; THAT'S ALREADY BEEN PROMISED. PRAY BIGGER. MAYBE THAT'S ALL GOD IS WAITING ON.

GEM:
THERE IS NO WASTED SEASON

The calling of Moses, to me, is one of the most powerful call stories in all of the Word of God. One of the things that I know about God is that when God issues a call, God calls the right person at the right time. For forty years Moses had lived in the courts of the Pharaohs. He was highly trained in the skills of the elite. He appeared to be destined for greatness, but now, he finds himself in a condition and context that is beneath what he seemed to be destined for. Moses now, as a result of a decision, finds himself banished to insignificance in the desert, where his companions are sheep and his prospects negligible. Moses makes a mistake and finds himself on the run. But forty years later, God visits Moses. In spite of the time that has gone by, God visits him. In spite of the wrong that he has done, God visits him. In spite of his solitude, God visits him. In spite of where he now finds himself, God visits him. When God has a plan for your life, it cannot be stopped because of one mistake. When you read the story of where Moses ends up and what he ends up doing, you will discover a powerful point. He is called to bring the people out of Egypt; which means he is called to shepherd the people. He is called to be a shepherd. When you see what he was doing when God finds him, you will see that what God calls him to do is something that he has been doing the whole time. The one who is to become the shepherd of God's people undergoes training in Midian. Can I tell you something? Nothing that you go through has been wasted time. Everything that God has allowed you to go through you went through to train you for the assignment God has on your life. Every person you have encountered; every place that you have been; every tear that you have cried—it was not wasted. God was training you for your destiny. God has been shaping your character through every circumstance and situation. God has been molding you through this season. I don't care what it is you are facing right now. Even if it seems you have gotten off track, I declare to you as you end this devotional the lesson I have learned in four months of confinement...THIS IS NOT A WASTED SEASON. WHEN GOD GETS THROUGH WITH THIS SEASON YOU WILL BE READY TO PRODUCE ON LEVELS YOU NEVER IMAGINED.

JUST BECAUSE YOU'RE BETTER OFF
DOES NOT ALWAYS MEAN YOU ARE
BETTER BLESSED. BE BETTER BLESSED
AND YOU WILL BE BETTER OFF.

DEVOTIONAL NOTES
Day 1

_____

_____

_____

_____

_____

_____

_____

_____

_____

_____

_____

_____

_____

_____

_____

_____

_____

_____

_____

_____

_____

_____

DEVOTIONAL NOTES
Day 2

_____

_____

_____

_____

_____

_____

_____

_____

_____

_____

_____

_____

_____

_____

_____

_____

_____

_____

_____

_____

_____

DEVOTIONAL NOTES
Day 3

_____

_____

_____

_____

_____

_____

_____

_____

_____

_____

_____

_____

_____

_____

_____

_____

_____

_____

_____

_____

_____

_____

DEVOTIONAL NOTES
Day 4

_____

_____

_____

_____

_____

_____

_____

_____

_____

_____

_____

_____

_____

_____

_____

_____

_____

_____

_____

_____

_____

_____

DEVOTIONAL NOTES
Day 5

_____

_____

_____

_____

_____

_____

_____

_____

_____

_____

_____

_____

_____

_____

_____

_____

_____

_____

_____

_____

_____

_____

_____

_____

DEVOTIONAL NOTES
Day 6

_____

_____

_____

_____

_____

_____

_____

_____

_____

_____

_____

_____

_____

_____

_____

_____

_____

_____

_____

_____

_____

_____

Devotional Notes
Day 7

_____

_____

_____

_____

_____

_____

_____

_____

_____

_____

_____

_____

_____

_____

_____

_____

_____

_____

_____

_____

_____

_____

DEVOTIONAL NOTES
Day 8

_____

_____

_____

_____

_____

_____

_____

_____

_____

_____

_____

_____

_____

_____

_____

_____

_____

_____

_____

_____

_____

DEVOTIONAL NOTES
Day 9

_____

_____

_____

_____

_____

_____

_____

_____

_____

_____

_____

_____

_____

_____

_____

_____

_____

_____

_____

_____

_____

_____

DEVOTIONAL NOTES
Day 10

_____

_____

_____

_____

_____

_____

_____

_____

_____

_____

_____

_____

_____

_____

_____

_____

_____

_____

_____

_____

_____

DEVOTIONAL NOTES
Day 11

_____

_____

_____

_____

_____

_____

_____

_____

_____

_____

_____

_____

_____

_____

_____

_____

_____

_____

_____

_____

_____

_____

DEVOTIONAL NOTES
Day 12

_____

_____

_____

_____

_____

_____

_____

_____

_____

_____

_____

_____

_____

_____

_____

_____

_____

_____

_____

DEVOTIONAL NOTES
Day 13

_____

_____

_____

_____

_____

_____

_____

_____

_____

_____

_____

_____

_____

_____

_____

_____

_____

_____

_____

_____

_____

DEVOTIONAL NOTES
Day 14

_____

_____

_____

_____

_____

_____

_____

_____

_____

_____

_____

_____

_____

_____

_____

_____

_____

_____

_____

_____

_____

_____

DEVOTIONAL NOTES
Day 15

_____

_____

_____

_____

_____

_____

_____

_____

_____

_____

_____

_____

_____

_____

_____

_____

_____

_____

_____

_____

_____

_____

DEVOTIONAL NOTES
Day 16

_____

_____

_____

_____

_____

_____

_____

_____

_____

_____

_____

_____

_____

_____

_____

_____

_____

_____

_____

_____

_____

DEVOTIONAL NOTES
Day 17

_____

_____

_____

_____

_____

_____

_____

_____

_____

_____

_____

_____

_____

_____

_____

_____

_____

_____

_____

_____

_____

DEVOTIONAL NOTES
Day 18

_____

_____

_____

_____

_____

_____

_____

_____

_____

_____

_____

_____

_____

_____

_____

_____

_____

_____

_____

_____

_____

_____

_____

_____

DEVOTIONAL NOTES
Day 19

_____

_____

_____

_____

_____

_____

_____

_____

_____

_____

_____

_____

_____

_____

_____

_____

_____

_____

_____

_____

_____

_____

DEVOTIONAL NOTES
Day 20

_____

_____

_____

_____

_____

_____

_____

_____

_____

_____

_____

_____

_____

_____

_____

_____

_____

_____

_____

_____

_____

_____

_____

DEVOTIONAL NOTES
Day 21

_____

_____

_____

_____

_____

_____

_____

_____

_____

_____

_____

_____

_____

_____

_____

_____

_____

_____

_____

_____

DEVOTIONAL NOTES
Day 22

_____

_____

_____

_____

_____

_____

_____

_____

_____

_____

_____

_____

_____

_____

_____

_____

_____

_____

_____

_____

_____

_____

_____

DEVOTIONAL NOTES
Day 23

_____

_____

_____

_____

_____

_____

_____

_____

_____

_____

_____

_____

_____

_____

_____

_____

_____

_____

_____

_____

_____

_____

_____

_____

DEVOTIONAL NOTES
Day 24

_____

_____

_____

_____

_____

_____

_____

_____

_____

_____

_____

_____

_____

_____

_____

_____

_____

_____

_____

_____

_____

_____

DEVOTIONAL NOTES
Day 25

_____

_____

_____

_____

_____

_____

_____

_____

_____

_____

_____

_____

_____

_____

_____

_____

_____

_____

_____

_____

_____

_____

DEVOTIONAL NOTES
Day 26

_____

_____

_____

_____

_____

_____

_____

_____

_____

_____

_____

_____

_____

_____

_____

_____

_____

_____

_____

_____

_____

_____

_____

DEVOTIONAL NOTES
Day 27

_____

_____

_____

_____

_____

_____

_____

_____

_____

_____

_____

_____

_____

_____

_____

_____

_____

_____

_____

_____

_____

_____

DEVOTIONAL NOTES
Day 28

_____

_____

_____

_____

_____

_____

_____

_____

_____

_____

_____

_____

_____

_____

_____

_____

_____

_____

_____

_____

_____

_____

_____

_____

DEVOTIONAL NOTES
Day 29

_____

_____

_____

_____

_____

_____

_____

_____

_____

_____

_____

_____

_____

_____

_____

_____

_____

_____

_____

_____

_____

Devotional Notes
Day 30

_____

_____

_____

_____

_____

_____

_____

_____

_____

_____

_____

_____

_____

_____

_____

_____

_____

_____

_____

_____

_____

_____

For More Information About
Bishop Rudolph McKissick, Jr's Ministry,
Visit:
www.NuggetsbyDayandGemsbyNight.com
www.Truth2PowerMinistries.org
www.Bethelite.org

E-mail Bishop McKissick at:
bishopmckjr@bethelite.org